Labrador Retrievers

By Maria Nelson

 **Gareth Stevens**
Publishing

Please visit our website, www.garethstevens.com. For a free color catalog of all our high-quality books, call toll free 1-800-542-2595 or fax 1-877-542-2596.

Library of Congress Cataloging-in-Publication Data

Nelson, Maria.
Labrador retrievers / Maria Nelson.
    p. cm. — (Great big dogs)
Includes index.
ISBN 978-1-4339-5784-0 (pbk.)
ISBN 978-1-4339-5785-7 (6-pack)
ISBN 978-1-4339-5782-6 (library binding)
1. Labrador retriever—Juvenile literature. I. Title.
SF429.L3N45 2011
636.752'7—dc22

2010046761

First Edition

Published in 2012 by
Gareth Stevens Publishing
111 East 14th Street, Suite 349
New York, NY 10003

Copyright © 2012 Gareth Stevens Publishing

Designer: Andrea Davison-Bartolotta
Editor: Kristen Rajczak

Photo credits: Cover, pp. 1, 5, 6, 13, 20 Shutterstock.com; p. 9 Kiko Iino/Getty Images; p. 10 iStockphoto/Thinkstock; p. 14 Mike Kemp/Getty Images; p. 17 altrendo images/ Getty Images; p. 18 Tim Sloan/AFP/Getty Images.

Printed in the United States of America

CPSIA compliance information: Batch #CS11GS: For further information contact Gareth Stevens, New York, New York at 1-800-542-2595.

Contents

Words in the glossary appear in **bold** type the first time they are used in the text.

Popular Breed

The Labrador retriever is one of the most popular dog **breeds**. As of 2009, it had been number one in the American Kennel Club's (AKC) ranking for 14 years! A retriever is a type of dog that goes and gets—or retrieves—things. There are many kinds of retrievers besides Labradors. There are golden retrievers, flat-coated retrievers, curly-coated retrievers, and many others.

Some Labs are show dogs or working dogs that help people who cannot do things themselves. Others are family pets.

4

Labs love to play with their owners.

5

Dog Tales

Labs can get bored easily. A bored Lab might dig holes in the yard or chew on your new shoes!

This Labrador retriever has become part of the family.

Labrador Love

Millions of American families have Labs. One of the things that has made Labs so popular is their loving nature. Labs are friendly. They're usually calm and don't get upset easily. Labs like to be around people. They'll play for hours and be gentle with little children.

Labs aren't good guard dogs. Although they have a loud bark, Labs like to make friends with everyone—even strangers!

Colorful Dog

Purebred Labrador retrievers are one of three colors: yellow, chocolate, or black. Yellow Labs range in color from reddish to almost white. Chocolate Labs are light to dark brown. Black Labs are black. Yellow and black Labs are more common than chocolate Labs.

Labs have a double coat. They have a short outer coat of stiff hairs. They also have a soft undercoat that keeps them dry and warm. Twice a year, Labs **shed** their coat.

Dog Tales

Puppies' colors depend on what color their parents are. A female Lab may be the mother of puppies that are different colors.

Whether black, chocolate, or yellow, Labs are always beautiful dogs.

Dog Tales
Labs aren't fully grown until they're 2 or 3 years old.

Labs are good swimmers. Their tails help them move through the water.

10

Big Fun

Labrador retrievers grow to be big dogs. They usually weigh between 55 and 75 pounds (25 and 34 kg) and are 21 to 24 inches (53 to 61 cm) tall at the shoulder. However, Labs love to eat! They can become overweight easily and reach 100 pounds (45 kg) or more.

It's easy to recognize a Lab by its otter-like tail. The tail is thick at the base and gets narrower at the end.

The Labrador Story

Labs were originally found in Newfoundland, Canada. They used to be called St. John's dogs in honor of the capital city, St. John's. They helped fishermen pull in fishing nets and caught fish that had gotten loose. In the 1800s, some were taken to England, where a few nobles kept the breed going.

The American Kennel Club officially recognized Labrador retrievers in 1917. In 1926, only 64 retrievers of all kinds were listed with the AKC. By 2001, there were 233,551 retrievers listed—165,970 of these were Labs!

Dog Tales

The **Earls** of Malmesbury in England bred many St. John's dogs in the 1800s. The third earl called the dogs "Labradors."

Many retriever breeds, like the Chesapeake Bay retriever on the left, look similar to Labs.

This Lab is retrieving a duck that has been shot by a hunter.

Hunting and Fishing

Labrador retrievers have always been working dogs. Labs' true retriever skills were recognized when their owners began to take them hunting. Labs retrieved small game for the hunter once it was shot down.

In Newfoundland, Labs were in the water a lot as they helped fishermen pull in nets. Labs must have been good at this job. They have **webbed** feet to help them swim. Labs' water-**repelling** coats stopped water from dripping into the boats when they climbed in.

Working Dog

Labrador retrievers are one of the most common breeds used as **service dogs**. Their kind nature makes them good companions for people who are lonely or sick. Labs also guide people who don't see or hear well. These Labs and their owners go through special training together.

Some Labs work with the police to find missing people. **Rescue** dogs use their sense of smell to find people lost in the snow, water, forests, or under rocks and soil.

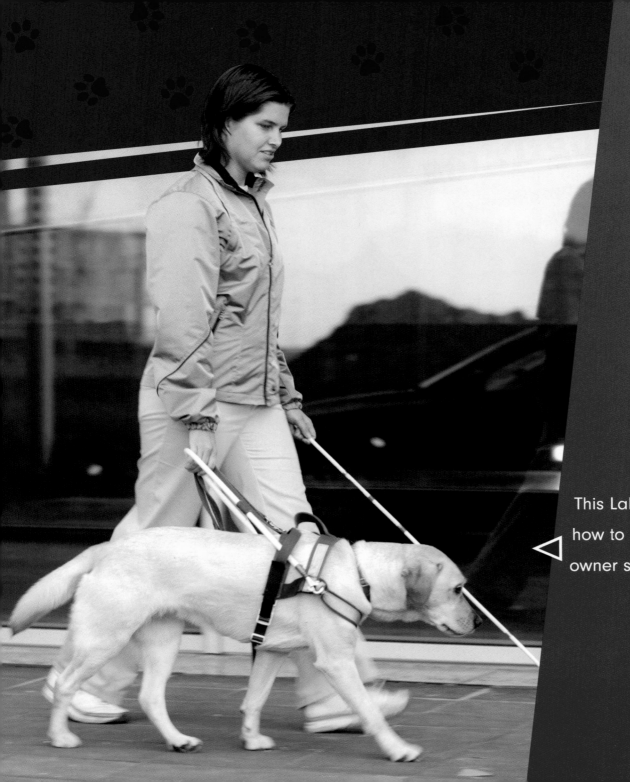

This Lab knows how to keep its owner safe.

17

Dog Tales

Twenty-two different dogs played Marley in the movie!

Buddy the chocolate Lab lived in the White House for more than 3 years!

18

Famous Labs

Many Labs have been in the spotlight over the years. Zeke the Wonder Dog is a Lab that does tricks during Michigan State University football games. There have been three "Zekes"—two yellow Labs and one black Lab.

President Bill Clinton and his family adopted a chocolate Lab and brought him to live at the White House. The dog's name was Buddy.

The troublemaking yellow Lab in the book and movie *Marley and Me* made yellow Labs even more popular.

Owning a Labrador Retriever

Labs are sweet dogs. However, they can get into trouble if they're not trained well. Labs need to know who's in charge.

Labs can get very excited. They need a lot of attention. Some Labs seem to have never-ending energy! A good way to keep your Lab happy is to take it for walks and play catch with it. They'll love just being with you!

Learning About Labs

height	21 to 24 inches (53 to 61 cm) at the shoulder
weight	55 to 75 pounds (25 to 34 kg)
coloring	yellow, chocolate, black
life span	10 to 12 years

Glossary

breed: a group of animals that share features different from other groups of the kind

earl: an English nobleman

purebred: an animal that has family members of only one breed

repel: to keep away

rescue: to free a person or thing from unsafe conditions

service dog: a dog that is trained to help people who do not hear, see, or move well

shed: to lose fur

webbed: joined by skin

Books

Landau, Elaine. *Labrador Retrievers Are the Best!* Minneapolis, MN: Lerner Publications, 2010.

Scheunemann, Pam. *Lovely Labrador Retrievers*. Edina, MN: ABDO Publishing, 2009.

Websites

The Labrador Retriever Club, Inc.
www.thelabradorclub.com
Learn more about the breed and activities of the club.

Woof! It's a Dog's Life
www.pbs.org/wgbh/woof
Play games and read stories about being a dog owner.

Publisher's note to educators and parents: Our editors have carefully reviewed these websites to ensure that they are suitable for students. Many websites change frequently, however, and we cannot guarantee that a site's future contents will continue to meet our high standards of quality and educational value. Be advised that students should be closely supervised whenever they access the Internet.

Index